PROSPERING
IN HARD TIMES
GUARANTEED
100%
TO CHANGE
YOUR LIFE
Your Blueprint for a life of Abundance & Surplus
Dr. Festus Adeyeye

Prospering In Hard Times

Paperback ISBN 978-0-9883707-8-4
eBook ISBN 978-0-9883707-9-1
Library of Congress Control Number 2013932752

Published by
GodKulture Publishing
Chicago, Illinois

Phone: 402-419-1072
Email: publishing@GodKulture.org
www.GodKulturepublishing.com

Transcriptions
Emilia Patterson

Editor-in-Chief
Titilola Akinyemi

Tree Photo by Goffaux Denis

Printed in the United States of America

Contents

Introduction

This book was birthed from an experience we had in our church in the year 2006. We experienced the relocation of some of our church members to other cities in the Southern and Midwestern areas of the United States. The war in Iraq took a serious toll on the American economy, which brought about inflation and a high cost of living. The prices of commodities such as gas rose astronomically throughout the country.

There was misinformation and a sense of apprehension that things were worse in New York City than in other places in the country, and the general impression was that living outside of New York City was better. This led some people in search of relief from the brunt of the "failing" economy to relocate to other places. The objective of this book is not to condemn or discourage anyone from relocating to wherever they are led; rather; it is to establish the fact that God has a set place for everyone in life, because our provisions and allocations are in our *divine* locations.

During this period, I was led by the Holy Spirit to teach and instruct our church members on how to prosper in hard times, thereby empowering them to bring their situations under control, and to live victoriously in the midst of economic hardship. In obedience to this, 2006 was one of the most prosperous years in our church. God blessed His work and His people prospered in every dimension of life. Giving to the work of God almost doubled and our church members experienced lifting more than any previous years.

While some people were busy complaining and subsequently relocating, God blessed those who knew how to "work their kingdom covenant." This book will make available to you those unchanging and unfailing principles that give us a lift in the midst of hardship. As you put these principles into practice, I know that you will be empowered to transform your destiny, the destinies of those around you, and that of the city in which you reside.

You have been created for dominion and you are neither a victim of circumstances nor a victim of a fluctuating economy. Dominion is your mandate; prosperity is your birthright; and abundance is your inheritance! Economies of the world may fluctuate, but you dance to a different tune and you have an inheritance preserved for you by the shed blood of Jesus Christ. Come with me on this adventure!

God's plan and purpose for His creations everywhere is that they prosper. "*And God blessed them and God said unto them, be fruitful and multiply and replenish the earth…*" He demonstrated His intention for mankind by positioning the first man, Adam, in the Garden of Eden. The Hebrew meaning of this garden is "Pleasant" or "Delight;" it was a prosperous place that abounded with mineral resources.

> *"And the Lord God planted a garden eastward in Eden: and there he put the man whom he had formed. And out of the ground made the Lord God to grow every tree that is pleasant to the sight, and good for food; the tree of life also in the midst of the garden, and the tree of knowledge of good and evil. And a river went out of Eden to water the garden, and from thence it was parted and become unto four heads"* [Genesis 2:8-15].

No matter the prevailing circumstances, the blessings of fruitfulness and multiplication are upon you so you can prosper and live a triumphant life. Thus, it is very vital to gain the understanding of how to translate these blessings into reality in our lives. Jesus Christ came so that we can prosper irrespective of where we live and irrespective of circumstances and situations.

> *"These things I have spoken unto you, that in me ye might have peace (wholeness, soundness of life). In this world ye shall have tribulation but be of good cheer; I have overcome the world"* [John 16:33, AMP].

You must be of good cheer and let it be ascertained in your heart that God is ready and able to bring stability into your life no matter the situation. This book is not a "Ten (10) Steps to Making Money," or a "Get Rich Quick Program" publication; it is a timely truth from God which will grant you Godly instructions on how to prosper at all times and also release an impartation for your breakthrough. This divine material will release wisdom into your life to enhance your much desired stability.

Chapter 1

This Too Shall Pass!!!

[Hard Times Are Not New]

(Ecclesiastes 1:9-11)

One way you can be easily defeated in life is to think that whatever you are going through is atypical or unique to you. Satan's objective is to convince you that victory has eluded you and that your situation is permanent and beyond repair. In order for us to be victorious, there are three fundamental truths we need to understand regarding hard times. These are the reality of hard times, the revelation of hard times, and the resolve for hard times.

THE REALITY OF HARD TIMES

Hard times are inevitable [1 Corinthians 10:13]. Historically and also from the testimonies of the scriptures, we know that hard times are common and that they are not new [Job 14:1]. It is recorded in the Bible that in the time of Abram there was a famine in the land and he went down to Egypt to sojourn there, "for the famine was grievous in the land" [Genesis 12:10]. Some other accounts of economic hard times can be seen in Genesis 26:1 (the time of Isaac), Genesis 47:13-14 (the time of Joseph), and 2 Kings 6:25 (the time of Elisha).

Over the years, America and other nations of the world have encountered recessions. Economies of nations will always be subjected to periods of "lows" and "highs." The same way that the climatic seasons of any region is subject to change; so also, hard times come and go. This may be as a result of a change of the times and the seasons, and the condition or the economy of the place where we dwell. It can also be as a result of human error, namely, our wrong choices, such as in the disobedience of Adam and the actions of the prodigal son.

Hard times can be caused by satanic attacks as was the case with Job. It can also be caused by the actions of mean people as seen in the case of Joseph's brother against Joseph, and Jezebel in the life of Prophet Elijah. Hard times can also be as a result of the call of God upon your life as seen in the life of David. The moment the anointing oil was poured on David's head as the next king, he became a target in the hands of the reprobate King Saul.

THE REVELATION OF HARD TIMES

We must not only recognize that hard times are not new, we must also understand that they are not permanent, depending on your reaction. Scripture corroborates the fact that God will not allow a believer to be confronted and tempted beyond what he or she can bear, and that He will also provide a means of escape out of the predicament. As Believers, we must realize that although hard times are not new, we do not have to experience living from one condition of hardship to another.

"The Lord knows the days of the upright: and their inheritance shall be forever. They shall not be ashamed in the evil time: ***and in the days of famine they shall be satisfied...*** *I have been young, and now am old, yet have I not seen the righteous forsaken, nor his seed begging bread"* [Psalm 37:17, 18, 25].

No matter how difficult things may be, you are not permitted to "go under" or to become a beggar. We can live victoriously and in abundance during this period. In every season of life, there is enough wisdom and grace in God to keep kingdom covenant practitioners above economic woes.

"But the God of grace who hath called us unto eternal glory by Christ Jesus, ***after you have suffered for a while*** *make you perfect, establish, strengthen, settle you"* [1 Peter 5:10].

You are not designed by God to suffer forever. You must be convinced that whatever you are going through now is for a season and the season will pass because every condition has an expiration period. So, as you read this book, prayerfully ask God to open your spiritual eyes so you can understand and embrace His provisions for you in this very season of your life because "THIS TOO SHALL PASS!"

THE RESOLVE FOR HARD TIMES

We receive our inheritance from God by faith. It is very vital for the believer to develop a mindset of conviction that he or she will not to be subdued and conquered by the difficulty of hard times. This is simply because your response to any season and time will depend upon your perception, which will ultimately determine an outcome of victory or defeat.

During His earthly ministry, Jesus demonstrated His authority over the forces of life including lack and famine. He fed five thousand with little or nothing. Provisions were made to enable Jesus to fulfill His earthly ministry. In the same manner, as Ambassadors of Christ on the earth, there is no economic force or distress that should prevent us from fulfilling the purpose of God for our lives.

Prophetically speaking, I hear the spirit of the Lord telling me that "this season too shall pass away" [2 Corinthians 2:14]. You must develop a winning mentality and a winning attitude based on the Word of God. In addition, you must resolve to engage in the practice of covenant principles that will terminate hard times and turn them into times of harvest. Indeed, there are covenant practices that if applied adequately, will turn seemingly difficult situations into dividends.

Chapter 2

El Shadai or "Men Shadai?"
[Kingdom Economics Vs. Human Economics]

It is very vital to develop the proper mindset for success and breakthrough in order to enjoy the best of the land, and that begins with personal knowledge of - and confidence in – the Person of God. When Abram (at age 99 years) was in doubt of the delivery of God's promise, God revealed Himself to him as the El Shadai; the Almighty God; the All Nourisher.

> *"And when Abram was ninety years old and nine, the Lord appeared to Abram and said unto him, I am the Almighty God; walk before me and be thou perfect. And I will make my covenant between me and thee, and will multiply thee exceedingly"* [Genesis 17:1-2].

Similarly, when Moses was unsure of the efficacy of his assignment, God revealed Himself to Moses as The Lord of the Earth, Yahweh [Exodus 6:2-8]. Your mindset must be governed by the ability of God as the All Sufficient, the Breasted One, who nourishes His children. As your ultimate source, you must believe by faith that there is no lack in Him and that He is able to generate all manner of resources. The economy of the land may be subjected to a period of hardship, but the economy of God says otherwise.

> *"If God will make windows in heaven, might these things be?"* [2 Kings 7:2].

The man on whose hand the king leaned failed to understand this principle. He was caught up in the natural and he forgot the supernatural dimension of abundance.

The government of the land and your earthly employees are never your sources. They are only channels through which God, the Ultimate Source chooses to flow or through which He manifests. God is the one and only source of all our blessings; all other avenues are channels. People, employers, governments, etc., can only be channels but never your source. When we connect with God, our ultimate source, He can speak to any channel for the provision of resources to us.

One of the lessons we learn during global recessions is that our help is not from Wall Street or from Main Street; our help is mainly from God and His Word. This is not to discount - or encourage a mentality of ignorance of - the validity of global market forces in determining the economic climate of any region. However, the truth still remains that God's economic force reigns supreme in the lives of kingdom covenant practitioners and over worldly economic forces. This is not an excuse for us to become arrogant and obnoxious to people or to develop an attitude of laziness. Cultivating healthy relationships with people is a must for our success at all times. The benefits of cultivating healthy relationships will be discussed in a later chapter.

My point however, is that our hope should not be in people or in the budget of the country you live in, or in the global economy. In conveying this point, I am not trying to be overly spiritual or unrealistic. **I understand that the economic conditions of our environment may have a bearing on our cost of living but it should not have a bearing on our way of living.** Living by the divine principles of God's kingdom will cause us to be catered for - and allow us to walk in abundance even in difficult times. Nevertheless, it is imperative that we have the right mindset; have the right focus; make the right decisions; and do the right things.

The questions I pose to you today are, "What kind of mindset do you have?" "Is your mindset allowing you to embrace the best of God or is it hindering you?" Governments come and go and so do their policies; but our God is the same yesterday, today, and forever. He is eternally constant in His ability and faithfulness. The global economic fluctuations or those of the country where you reside do not constitute fluctuations in God's ability.

> *"Thy raiment waxed not old upon thee, neither did thy foot swell, these forty years"* [Deuteronomy 8:4].

God ensured that the Israelites were adequately provided for in the wilderness where nothing was supposed to thrive; He gave them food to eat and, their raiment never waxed old.

> *"And there was a great famine in Samaria, and behold they besieged it, until a donkey's head was sold for eighty shekels of silver, and a fourth of a kab of dove's dung for five shekels of silver. As the king of Israel was passing by upon the wall a woman cried out to him, saying help my Lord O king. And he said, 'If the lord does not help thee, whence shall I help thee? Out of the barn floor or out of the winepress?'"*
> [2 Kings 6:25-27].

In the scenario above, human economics failed and the kings became helpless. No matter how wise or smart human beings are, there are limits to their wisdom. I am convinced that in God's wisdom He sometimes allows us to come to the end of our human effort in order for us to absolutely depend upon Him. For example, I have observed that tragic situations in America, such as shootings in our schools and malls – behaviors and attacks that are definitely satanic - usually generate an unusual hunger for God and prayer. It is common to see Churches filled with people who might not have been to church in many years.

Governmental policies are usually more open and receptive to faith-based initiatives to complement governmental outreach to the people. In essence, in the face of such evil, the nation as a whole suddenly comes to the realization of the futility of relying only on military and monetary power to the exclusion of the one and true God.

"BY THIS TIME TOMORROW…" [A Word from God will Change the Course of Your Destiny]

In the midst of the severe conditions in Samaria, God sent Prophet Elisha with a word for the people:

> *"Then Elisha said, Hear the word of the Lord. Thus says the Lord:* ***by this time tomorrow*** *a measure of flour will be sold for a shekel and two measures of barley for a shekel in the gate of Samaria"* [2 Kings 7:1].

One word from God can - and will - turn your life around. No matter the severity of your condition, the Word of God is potent enough to bring about a turnaround for good. We live in a world full of skeptics and we are always surrounded by all kinds of depressing news. These can demoralize us and even breed fear, doubt, and depression. You cannot afford to expose yourself to information that will instill fear into your spirit. Of course you need to listen to the news and keep yourself abreast of the happenings around you. However, ensure that your spirit is not governed by information only. Learn to process information by subjecting it to the Word of God, using faith as a shield to protect your mind from the fiery darts of the enemy.

DON'T PANIC!

If unchecked, the initial human reaction to any abnormal situation is to panic, fret or be overly anxious. If you intend to walk in faith and victory, hard times are not the times to panic or to be anxious. They are not the times or seasons to run helter skelter. It is also not the time for our hearts to faint. If we allow the manifestations of the hard times to gain control of our spirit man, we will begin to agitate and make irrational decisions like the women mentioned in 2 Kings 6:28, who made the decision to eat their children during their hard times.

> *"And the king said unto her, what ails thee? And she answered, this woman said unto me, give thy son that we may eat him today, and we will eat my son tomorrow. So we boiled my son, and did eat him: and I said unto her on the next day, Give thy son, that we may eat him: and she hath hid her son"*
> [2 Kings 6:28-29].

Unknown to these women, God already programmed an abundance of wealth and food for the inhabitants of their city; it was just a matter of days before the manifestation of the divine provisions. Unfortunately, the woman already ate her child. **Whenever you panic, you are bound to make wrong assumptions that will lead to wrong decisions.** Sometimes, such decisions could be costly, irreversible, and even deadly.

What is your condition at this moment? God is saying through the pages of this divine material and through His spirit today, "Fear not; be still and know that I am God" [Psalm 46:11]. This is not to say that you should not be concerned about your life or that you should develop a carefree attitude. Rather, you must learn to see things from God's perspective. Instead of fretting and agonizing, you need to set yourself in agreement with kingdom principles and position yourself for kingdom abundance.

THE GOD OF EXTREMES

"By this time tomorrow a measure of barley will be sold for a shekel…" What an extreme move from absolute famine to total abundance! In God's modus operandus, He speaks of divine healing when a man's hope of recovery is gone and he is awaiting death. God speaks of abundance in the midst of lack and insufficiency. God speaks of salvation and deliverance when a person is hell-bound. God speaks of hope in the midst of hopeless conditions. Whatever condition you are in now, be rest assured that God's thoughts and ways are totally different from that of man. The Word of God is the container of His power and breakthrough.

> *"He sent forth his word, and healed them, and delivered them from their destructions"* [Psalms 107:20].

God's Word is God's method! If you want to know how God works, locate His Words. God does nothing outside of His Word. His Words are His ways and His methods. God does not go around; He only sends his Words around. You need to value His Words and feed on them because therein lies your next dimension.

> *"Neither have I gone back from the commandment of his lips: I have esteemed the words of his mouth more than my necessary food"* [Job 23:13].

Place a high value on God's Word more than anyone or any situation. The way to pursue God in order to embrace His provision is to pursue His Words. Comprehending the Words of God is comprehending God, and knowing the Words of

God is knowing God. Everything you want to obtain from God is channeled through His Words. God is His Word and His Word is Him. You need Word revelation in order to secure material restoration, since the former sets the pace for the latter. Your healing, deliverance, and prosperity all become a reality when you can see them first in the Word. God makes all things by His Words and He upholds all things by His Words. If anything is damaged and cannot be humanly fixed, God restores it by His Words.

I was conducting a ministration at a church in North Carolina, in July 2010. Towards the end of the service, God, by a word of knowledge spoke through me and revealed the condition of a man suffering from kidney malfunction. Unbeknownst to me, there was indeed a man at the back of the huge auditorium who had been diagnosed with terminal renal disease and was on dialysis. He was assisted to the front of the auditorium by two people and hands were laid on him. I prayed over him in the name of Jesus and asked God to perfect His healing covenant in the man's life. Exactly two weeks later, the host pastor of that church sent a testimony by email that the man was completely healed and was able to perform renal functions for the first time in years, without the need for dialysis.

The good news is that his healing is permanent; to date, he is still off dialysis. Blessed be the name of the Lord for His grace and mercy. If a Physician advises you that nothing more can be done about your situation, crying is impractical. Rather, go to God who has replacement parts! I am glad to let you know that God still sends His Word out for restoration and healing.

Put your trust in God's Word because it cannot be shaken. The financial market may fluctuate and military and mortgage influences may be uncertain, but do not be alarmed; God's Word remains unchangeable.

> *"Heaven and earth shall pass away, but my words shall not pass away"* [Matthew 24:35].

The Word of God is also the container of God's wisdom. To excel and to walk in abundance at all times including hard times requires divine wisdom.

> *"They that be wise shall shine as the brightness of the firmament; and they that turn many to righteousness as the stars for ever and ever"* [Daniel 12:3].

For every human challenge, there is a divine wisdom solution. Divine wisdom does not just provide answers, it also creates answers. So whatever can be created at all times is within the range of wisdom.

> *"The Lord by wisdom has founded the earth; by understanding hath he established the heaven"* [Proverbs 3:19].

God's wisdom is made available to us as we read, meditate, reflect and ruminate on His Words. Divine wisdom will deliver heavenly ideas into your life which will cause you to excel in the midst of hardship. In Genesis 41, a word of wisdom from Joseph to Pharaoh shifted the economy of

Egypt from scarceness to surplus. Joseph was elevated in a strange land because of the manifestations of wisdom. As you prayerfully study God's Word, you will come into contact with divine wisdom that will lift you above your peers and beyond your time. Wisdom is the principal thing that makes principal men.

Chapter 3

Covenant of Wealth
[The Basis for Our Prosperity]

CORPORATE MERGING

"Corporate Merging" is a very familiar term in the corporate world. This is a term that describes a situation whereby a company that is becoming weak economically or dwindling in profits merges with a very progressive or vibrant one in other to ride on the strength of the progressive company. Likewise, God can be considered as our Corporate Partner.

At the onset of receiving Christ in salvation, we automatically become joint heirs with Christ and to His inheritance. We are joined with God who is stronger and abundant in resources. He, therefore, comes in His strongest capacity as the "I AM" God and forms a covenant partnership with you and me. So where we are weak, He is strong, and where we are lacking, He is full of abundance.

As believers, we need to be cognizant of our covenant relationship with God through the shed blood of Jesus Christ. One of the vital ingredients for prospering in hard times is having the proper understanding of the working knowledge of our kingdom covenant relationship with God. Prospering at all times is not a bargain, neither is it by luck or by chance; it begins with God and His covenant with us. Kingdom covenant will always prevail! God is bound by His covenant and honors every element of it.

> *"My covenant will I not break, nor alter the thing that is gone out of my lips"* [Psalms 89:34].

Therefore as God's children, we cannot live our lives based on circumstances but rather, on obedience to God's Word, His Plan, and His Promises.

BE COVENANT DRIVEN

Many Christians today are circumstances-driven, thereby allowing them to be distracted or discouraged by circumstances. Some have even entertained governance by the prevailing conditions around them. Despite the prevailing famine in the time of Abraham, God caused him to increase and he became rich in silver, cattle and gold. Isaac in obedience to God stayed and invested (sowed) in the land when most people "checked out of town." As a result, he received a hundred-fold return in the same year, even with the scorching heat of the waterless desert.

> *"And the man waxed great and went forward, and grew until he became very great"* [Genesis 26:13].

Covenant works at all times! If famine could not stop our covenant fathers then famine cannot stop us. It has been written that there is no place on this planet earth where there are no lenders and borrowers, beggars and givers. What's more, they all live in the same environment. It therefore begs the questions, "Why is this so?" "Where did the lender get his excess?" Stop looking at shadows and allow divine covenant to govern your thinking.

The truth you embrace in your hearts is very vital because it will not only determine how you perceive yourself, it will also determine the extent to which you can receive the promises of God. For instance, God delivered the land of Canaan to the Israelites but they did not enter in and possess it due to the report by the ten spies, in which they perceived themselves as grasshoppers; a report that was based on unbelief.

Caleb and Joshua on the other hand were able to see themselves not as ordinary men, but as covenant carriers. Due to their accurate perception, they were able to take hold of the promises of God and what others saw as obstacles, Caleb and Joshua saw as great opportunities for advancement. At the age of 85, Caleb inherited the promise of God to secure the Promised Land, while several million Israelites wandered and died in the wilderness because of unbelief and wrong perceptions. You must be scripturally informed and desire to know God and your inheritance in Christ. Christianity goes beyond being religious, to having a walk with God that is based solely on kingdom covenant. Jesus came as a mediator of a better covenant based on better promises.

> *"But now hath obtained a more excellent ministry, by how much also he is the mediator of a better covenant, which was established upon better promises"* [Hebrews 8:6].

Kingdom economy and the economy of the land obey two separate laws. The economy of the land obeys the law of nature and the law of sin and death and it has no bearing on our covenant walk. On the other hand, kingdom economy, which is based on covenant, obeys the law of the spirit of life in Christ Jesus. We as believers are spirit beings and we are not to be controlled and governed by natural circumstances.

> *"He that comes from above is above all: he that is of the earth is earthly, and speaks of the earth: he that comes from heaven is above all"* [John 3:31].

People are not down because things are down; they are down because they do not have the light (revelation) to be up. What we need is the light of God's Word which will enable us to rise up at all times. Since this covenant is everlasting and cannot be broken, there is no economic condition that can alter the plan of God for our lives or the things that He has said about us. Sit tight, engage your covenant, and make it work for you!

Chapter 4

Thriving God's Way
[Journeying into Your Wealthy Place]

"Beloved, I pray that you may prosper in all things and be in health, just as your soul prospers [3 John 1:2].

God desires that we experience His blessing in its entirety. However, it is the prosperity of our soul that energizes the prosperity of the total man, and the human soul thrives only when God's Word takes root in it. Thus, our daily decisions are influenced by a productive thought pattern. When our decisions and actions line up with the will of God, we are on course to the fulfillment of destiny and will be able to prosper at all times.

As we align with the life God intended for us, He gladly provides for us. This may not happen overnight; it may require a process and there are laws governing such processes, namely physical and spiritual laws. The physical law directs all activities on earth but the spiritual law is superior to the physical laws; in fact, the former gives birth to the latter.

> *"By faith we understand that the worlds were framed by the word of God, so that the things which are seen were not made of things which are visible"* [Hebrews 11:3].

True prosperity is the ability to use God's power to meet the needs of mankind. God used the nation of Israel as a case study for us to follow, if we want to experience His notion of prosperity. The Israelites lived in Egypt as slaves; nevertheless, they were freed by God's supernatural power. Despite the fact that they were physically delivered from bondage, they left Egypt with a "slavery mentality" because they neither owned anything nor did they ever expect any form of abundance. On the contrary, God expected them to start thinking differently, since they were to conquer and inhabit the land of Canaan. A different thought process was imperative to the commencement of a new walk with God that would lead to abundance.

God did not want them to become solely dependent on the daily manna that was provided for their sustenance in the wilderness. His desire was that they would develop a mentality and a lifestyle of trust and obedience on God for abundance. The miracle of simply walking out each morning to pick up (the provision of) manna, stopped. Now, they were expected to plow the ground, plant seeds, and harvest before they could eat. They were also to keep some seeds for planting the next season in order to continue this process.

The Promised Land was described figuratively as a land flowing with milk and honey. Nevertheless, also figuratively, to obtain the milk, it is expected that one must know how to rear cattle and milk them. And to obtain the honey, one must also know how to handle bees for the creation of honeycombs. Entering and thriving in the Promised Land demanded hard work based on faith in God. The Israelites' journey is no different from that which present day believers must embark upon to arrive at their wealthy place and the requisite principles are no different from those identified below.

SACRIFICIAL SEED FAITH GIVING

God is no respecter of persons but a respecter of principles. Principles are universal laws that govern human existence. Spiritual or natural principles always work for whoever works them. One of such principles is "seed faith giving."

> *"Gather My saints together to Me, Those who have made a covenant with Me by sacrifice. Those who sow in tears shall reap in joy. He who continually goes forth weeping, Bearing seed for sowing, Shall doubtless come again with rejoicing, Bringing his sheaves with him"* [Psalm 50:5, 126:5-6].

Sacrificial giving is a remarkable master key for prospering at all times. Your ability to prosper at any time does not depend on what you do not have but on what you are willing to give sacrificially. Many give, but only a select few give sacrificially. Some give sacrificially once in a while, but very few do it consistently. Living a life of sacrificial giving keeps your heaven perpetually open. Sacrificial giving is based solely upon the law of sowing and reaping.

SOWING & REAPING

There is one law that has outlasted every other law in existence. It is a law that precedes the Ten Commandments that God gave the children of Israel. It is one law that is as certain as any other law; it is the law of sowing and reaping, which produces results that are predictable as long as the earth remains.

> *"While the earth remains, Seedtime and harvest, Cold and heat, winter and summer, and day and night shall not cease"* [Genesis 8:22].

Sowing and reaping can teach us a lot about life and God's plan to prosper us in the kingdom. This is why Jesus uses agricultural terms a significant number of times in the gospel, to explain this truth. God wants us to understand that this simple rule will guide our productivity and will also affect the way He relates with us. The seed of any crop is the most valuable asset in the hand of a farmer because therein exists the potential for his desired harvest. In the same manner, Christians must value the power of the seed. Every desired harvest is located inside a seed that must be sown.

Therefore, if we desire to live life the way God intended, we must build our lives like a farmer would. We must approach all that we do the way a farmer will go about his business. We must believe that as long as we sow the right seed, surely there will be a reaping of the right harvest. Below are some of the laws of sowing and reaping we must understand and apply, in order to enjoy continuous prosperity.

(1) Be Careful How You Sow. This law is best summed up with the statement *"He who sows sparingly will reap sparingly"* [2 Corinthians 9:6]. The pattern here is that you only reap whatever you sow. Your harvest will have the same nature as your seed. If you have a precious seed that you desire to reproduce, sow it so that God can multiply it. When Jesus wanted to feed the multitudes, He only needed five loaves and two small fishes as seed, and yet the crowd was well taken care of, and there were leftovers.

(2) Be Careful Where You Sow. Every good farmer knows that where he sows is as important as what he sows. The texture of the soil has to measure up to the potential of the seed. Similarly, we have to be conscious of the environment in which we sow our seeds. It is of utmost importance that we release our seed into good ground [Mark 4:8]. It is our responsibility to locate a good ground, which can be a flourishing ministry where we derive our spiritual nourishment or a spiritual leader whose grace is beneficial to our lives. This is necessary because the ground determines the quality of our harvest and how soon the seeds are multiplied back to us.

(3) Be Careful When You Sow. There is a time and a season for everything [Ecclesiastes 3:1]. A farmer knows that some seeds only germinate in the rainy season while too much water can destroy other types of seeds. Wisdom demands that we utilize opportune times as set by the Holy Spirit for specific seed sowing. Even though we can sow anytime, some opportunities come in seasons. Sometimes, God will open certain opportunities for sowing which He intends to use for a desired harvest that we have prayed about. It is therefore important for us to be discerning so that we do not miss out.

(4) Do Not Eat Your Seed. If a farmer ate all his crops including the seed, he might as well kiss farming and harvest goodbye. A farmer must learn to retain seeds for the next year of farming. We must be prudent in our finances and learn not to consume everything we acquire. The Bible says an unwise man spends it all [Proverbs 21:20]. A portion of our income should be set aside as seed so that we can be prepared for an opportune moment to sow, in order to have a continuous cycle of harvest.

(5) No Matter What, Continue Sowing. A farmer knows the importance of always bouncing back. He does not allow poor results from a previous year of farming to affect the potential of another year. Even if all you are able to harvest in a particular year is not encouraging, keep sowing because the scripture tells us:

> "*…let us not be weary in well doing: for in due season we shall reap, if we faint not*" [Galatians 6:9, KJV].

The power of multiplication is in your hands. The seed you hold will grow and increase if it is planted and nurtured, since only what you sow can multiply. If you eat it, it is gone; if you sow it, it will come back many times more, just as God gave His Son as a seed for the harvest of millions of souls into His Kingdom.

Your sowing determines your reaping. You order your harvest in advance by the seeds you plant, and so, your future is in your hand. You decide your tomorrow by your sowing today. God will not be mocked. This is an unchangeable principle designed to bless those who live in God's kingdom.

TITHES

This is another means of prospering that is based on obedience to the principle of sacrificial giving. Tithing means giving a tenth of all income to God faithfully and continuously. This ten percent belongs to God; we are only giving it back to Him.

> *"Bring all the tithes into the storehouse, That there may be food in My house, And try Me now in this," Says the Lord of hosts, "If I will not open for you the windows of heaven And pour out for you such blessing That there will not be room enough to receive it. And I will rebuke the devourer for your sakes, So that he will not destroy the fruit of your ground, Nor shall the vine fail to bear fruit for you in the field," Says the Lord of hosts"* [Malachi 3:10-11].

The scripture above outlines the blessings of tithing, as well as the consequences of not tithing. Tithing is a covenant practice that redeems the remaining ninety percent we have and also unfolds great blessings upon us.

In many churches, people are told that when they give their tithes, God will open the windows of heaven and pour them a blessing. As a result, many fold their hands waiting for God to miraculously and immediately resolve their problems.

While this can occur, it is not the usual course of action. The blessing that has been poured on us is the supernatural empowerment that multiplies the seed(s) that we plant. The blessing opens up channels of opportunities, favor connections, and supernatural doors that would not have been open otherwise. It is our responsibility to step through the open doors in order to maximize divine moments for prosperity.

Chapter 5

Beyond Tithes and Offerings

"But thou shall remember the Lord thy God: for it is he that giveth thee power to get wealth, that He may establish his covenant which he sware unto thy fathers" [Deuteronomy 8:18].

As stated earlier, one of the reasons why God desires our prosperity is so that His covenant can be fulfilled. From this scripture, we should take note that there are two distinct factors involved in the journey to prosperity. There is the "power," the God-factor, and there is "to get" wealth, the human factor. God gives us power but He does not give us wealth or money. Power means enablement, ability, favor, and opportunities.

For a long time, the Church has failed to teach this truth on prospering in the Kingdom of God. We have been taught that all we have to do as Christians is to give our tithes, be faithful, avoid sin, attend Church Services, and we will prosper! There are Christians who believe so much in this teaching that they almost expect angels to deposit money under their pillows when they are sleeping! This is not a balanced teaching and

God is changing this erroneous mindset. What God does is to grant us the enablement. For instance, God will not open a company for us but He can place the desire in our hearts, open the proper channels, and grant us the right connections; however, it is up to us to piece the logistics together, practically. You may give your tithes, be faithful, fast and pray and yet remain poor if this fundamental truth is not applied.

Does this mean that we should not tithe and live holy? The answer of course is an emphatic "No!" Paying your tithes, being obedient and walking faithfully with God all provide the spiritual foundation for our prosperity. Wisdom however, demands that you build upon the foundation for a prosperous outcome.

THE WINDOWS OF HEAVEN

God promises to open the windows of Heaven and pour down His blessings. However, this does not mean that God will send dollars or any other currency from Heaven. Windows as we know are placed in houses to provide illumination and fresh air. In providing illumination, God will open our eyes of understanding and give us creative ideas, wisdom and opportunities. When we remain faithful in the practice of tithing and in our walk with God, He will deposit godly ideas in our spirit man that will cause us to prosper in any season. In providing fresh air, God provides us with totally balanced prosperity, meaning that He will give us the peace of mind, the long life and the good health to enjoy what we have.

Power in the scripture above means that God will give us opportunities, connections and relationships that will enhance our ability to prosper. No matter the circumstances of life or the climate or environment we live in, opportunities abound, always. Our focus should be geared towards making the transfer of such opportunities into our lives.

MAKING THE TRANSFER

In the time of famine and difficulty God gave a word through prophet Elijah in 2 Kings 7. The Word of God ended the famine by opening a channel; the Word of God created abundance in the camp of the Syrians on the other side of town.

> *"And there were four leprous men at the entering in of the gate: and they said one to another, why sit we here until we die? If we say, we will enter the city, then the famine is in the city, and we shall die there: and if we sit still here, we die also. Now therefore come, and let us fall unto the host of the Syrians: if they save us alive, we shall live; and if they kill us, we shall but die"* [2 Kings 7:3-4].

However, it took the faith actions of the four lepers to effect the transfer of the bounties from the Syrian camp to the Israelites.

God is the one who gives opportunities and He is still in the business of doing so. As stated in the Bible, God has set before us an open door; that is to say, God gives opportunities that are unrestricted and access that no one can impede. Even as of now, there are opportunities to be blessed; opportunities to prosper, to become a millionaire; and to increase on all sides.

SEEDED WITH GREATNESS

> *"For the kingdom of heaven is likened unto a man traveling into a far country who called his own servants, and delivered unto them his goods. And unto one he gave five talents, to another two, and to another one;* ***to every man according to his several ability;*** *and straightway took his journey"*
> [Matthew 25:14-15].

Another dimension that guarantees perpetual breakthrough is the seed of talents, abilities and gifts ingrained inside every person. Even the homeless individual on the street is seeded with greatness. There is a glorious deposit inside each and every one of us, which when discovered and utilized, will institute his or her throne on the earth. It is the seed for your lifting and it forms the basis for prospering at all times.

God knows exactly what you need for your shining and breakthrough and He has already made a divine deposit *in you!* When you discover and utilize your God-given talents, gifts, and abilities, it guarantees you a place at the pinnacle. So one of the easiest ways to overcome frustration and to prosper at any given time is to recognize the divine deposit that is on your inside. Irrespective of where you are at any given point in time, be it in a ministerial capacity, or in business, or at your place of work, when you discern and begin to operate your God-given proficiencies, exceptional results are inevitable, because you are already graced for it.

Not only does God know what you need and provides it for you, He also gives you what you can easily handle. There are no divine deposits without divine recipients. **Whatever God by grace has deposited in you can also be retrieved by you, in grace.**

> *"I am what I am by the grace of God"* [1 Corinthians 15:10].

You do not have to envy anyone in life for whatever measure of success they are enjoying, because God has graced you to revel in your own breakthrough and prosperity. Everybody has "a measure!"

> *"And to one he gave five talents, to another two, and to another one, to each according to his own ability"* [Matthew 25:15].

Even the man with one talent received something of value from his master. The things in our lives that may seem insignificant are not to be taken for granted. My question to you today is "What is it that you know God has graced you to do?" Instead of coveting what others have, start utilizing what God has given unto *you!*

God is not into equal distribution of wealth, but He is into equal distribution of opportunities; there is a seed in you! Every seed has the capability of becoming the kind of plant or tree that produced it. In other words, though small, the seed has all the potentialities of a tree and will become a tree in the future. Similarly, you are not empty because there is a seed that God placed in you at creation. That seed is the seed of your greatness; it is the seed of accomplishment. When given the opportunity to express itself, that seed enables you to achieve whatever you want to achieve in life. You cannot afford to live and die small when all it takes to be great lies within you. Think big and see yourself becoming great. Look inwards and draw out the power to move forward. Everyone came into this world fully loaded with abilities that are so designed to enable him or her achieve all he or she could ever dream of achieving in life.

The true worth of every man is the measure of the gifts, talents and potential he possesses. It is neither a measure of his savings nor his investments, nor yet his affluence; it is the sum total of the resources in him! For any man to become distinguished in life, he must come to the realization of his full potential and tap into such with maximum effort. You were born to reign, dominate and be in-charge, and you can only achieve this by diligently exploring all of the possibilities that lie within you. You could not have been made any better than you were made. The problem is not with your make-up; the problem is not with where you were born; the problem is not with the family into which you were born, poor or rich; the problem is in you ascertaining who you are as well as the several abilities deposited into you at creation.

DISCERNING TALENTS, GIFTS AND CALLINGS

Prospering at all times is strongly dependent upon your discernment of your talents, gifts and callings.

TALENTS

Everyone has at least one talent given to him by God. One of the reasons why some people have not experienced the vision of God for their lives is that they are consumed by what is happening in other people's lives. If you do not know who you are, people will impose "who you are not," on you.

What is a talent? A talent is an innate ability; it is a natural endowment; it is something you are born with; it is what makes you a unique entity. It is your differential factor because if you are not different, you are not needed. It can also be described as something you have a flair for; something you do with ease; something you excel in doing; something you are just naturally inspired to do well. For example, there are people who sing with ease; and then there are those who attend music school for five years and still do not know how to sing. There are those who attended culinary schools but whose food will cause a restaurant to close down due to a lack of appeal. Yet, there are those who did not attend any culinary school but through innate ability will cook scrumptious meals.

Likewise, there are those who have the flair for sports and have mastered the techniques of sportsmanship. There are some individuals that whatever product they choose to sell, sells as a result of innate talent for business. There are equally people who are not business-savvy, but are hardworking employees who truly earn their wages. What is it that gets you excited and has value for prosperity? You can soar high and be lifted above your circumstances by identifying your talent(s).

GIFTS

What is a gift? A gift can be described as a combination of developed talents and skills or developed talents and relevant qualitative education or training; in essence, expertise. You become a gifted person by honing your skills and taking ownership of your talents through relevant training. For example, if you have a flair for cooking, you may choose to undergo culinary training to become an expert.

In a decent society, people are guided from their youth on the path to the development of their talents. Realizing he had the talent to speak at the age of four years, Robert H. Schuller, (American Televangelist, Pastor and Motivational Speaker), developed this talent into a gift and in the process it became a calling. Daniel, Shadrack, Meshack and Abednego by divine endowment, excelled in wisdom, knowledge, and the capability for learning new skills. The Babylonian king placed them in school (among his most trusted wise men and counselors) and they became ten times better than Babylonian (Chaldean) magicians, soothsayers, and astrologers. Identify your talents and base your training on that talent. Your talent is given form and shape through learning, to turn it into a gift.

CALLINGS

> *"For the gifts and calling of God are without repentance"* [Romans 11:29].

What is a call? A call is a divine selection and appointment for a special assignment. There are certain things God has called certain individuals to do that others are not called to do. It is beyond talents and also beyond gifts and although it centers on ministry, it is not limited to ministry.

> *"But when it pleased God, who separated me from my mother's womb, and called me by his grace"* [Galatians 1:15].

There are examples of men and women who were specifically called into certain domains of life beyond the ministry and they prospered as a result of yielding to their calling. Nehemiah was called with special grace as a statesman. Martin Luther King was also called among many things to steer the heart of America away from the injustice of racism. The Reformer John Knox prayed, *"Give me Scotland or I die!"* No wonder Mary, Queen of Scots, declared that she was more afraid of John Knox's prayers than of an army of ten thousand. She recognized the potency of a spiritual revolution over and above any military or political power.

A person's calling usually comes with special grace from God for accomplishment. God does not call us based upon our aptitude, gifts, and talents, but He still uses them to aid our calling. David was a shepherd when God called him and his experience with the cattle became handy as the shepherd of Israel. What God designs you for is what he assigns you to do. Do not try to shoulder the burdens for which you are not designed. When you locate your calling, it causes you to prosper in your season.

You flourish easily in any season when you focus your energy on who and what you are and the tasks God has assigned to you. **In God's kingdom people do not win by doing what they are capable of doing, but by doing what they are assigned to do**. You will surely prosper either by identifying your talents and gifts or by receiving a call from God, each of which can only be accessed through the help of the Holy Spirit. Connection with the person of the Holy Spirit helps you to avoid the deception of the devil and makes you adept at recognizing the plan of God for your life.

Chapter 6

Practical Lessons for Prosperity

[Lessons from the Animals]

As exemplified in Proverbs 30:24-28, there are fundamental lessons to be gleaned from the lives of the ants, conies, locusts, and spiders.

> *"There be four things which are little upon the earth; but they are exceeding wise: The ants are a people not strong, yet they prepare their meat in the summer, The conies are but a feeble folk, yet make they their houses in the rocks; The locust have not king, yet go they forth all of them by bands; The spider takes hold with her hands, and is in Kings' palaces"*
> [Proverbs 30:24-28].

The sentences above speak of the following:

1. Foresight and Planning.
2. Divine Habitat - Utilizing what you have, where you are.
3. Partnership - Leveraging Relationships.
4. Creativity and Diligence.

LESSONS FROM THE ANTS

> *"The ants are a people not strong, yet they prepare their meat in the summer…"* [Proverbs 30:25].

Although the ants are feeble and weak, we are admonished in Proverbs 6:6 to "go to the ant, consider her ways, and be wise." Why does God want us to learn from the ants? It is quite simple - the ants impress upon us, the importance of foresight and the value of preparation.

FORESIGHT

Wealth belongs to those who have foresight. These are the people who can envisage and plan their future at the present time, and who do not live for immediate gratification.

In every civilization and generation, there are those whose philosophy only focuses on immediate gratification without any regard for the future. Foresight enables one to anticipate the future and proactively take certain profitable actions that others will not. It also helps to avoid the mindset of those that I refer to as the "faith fatalists." The "faith fatalist" philosophy is that "what will be, will be;" that is, "everything is in the hands of a 'Higher Power.'" This philosophy is not only incorrect but it is detrimental to our lives and destinies. If whatever will be will be, then what is the purpose of seeking and asking in prayer? [Matthew 7:7-9]. If whatever will be will be, what is the essence of the law of sowing and reaping? [Galatians 6:7].

If the outcome of our lives has already been set, why would Jesus ask us to pray for the will of God to be done on the earth as it is in heaven? Why would God seek a man to stand in the gap for mankind so He could carry out His purpose? [Ezekiel 22:30]. This is simply because in order for God to get involved with us on earth, He needs man's active participation. In order for God to get involved in your life, He requires your active participation and your earthly initiation.

> *"The heaven, even the heavens are the Lord's: but the earth hath he given to the children of men"* [Psalms 115:16].

God is in control of your life to the extent that you have invited Him to be. Therefore, you need to carefully agree with God to map a plan for your future through foresight and preparation – just like the ants. Opportunities abound irrespective of times and seasons and even during hard times, but we must be prepared to appropriate them.

PLANNING

Never allow lack to place a limitation on you. **It is not what you lack that dictates your future success but your ability to harness the opportunities life affords at present.** Therefore, what we do with the opportunities that come our way is what will determine our success or failure. Just like the ant lacks strength, everyone has one deficit or the other, so insufficiency should not form the basis for any excuse or be used as a crutch. The ant takes charge of her future and takes responsibility for her life. The ant does not allow any circumstance or limitation to hinder her success; she is always ready and prepared.

Preparation means to make something or someone ready for a future occurrence, just as the ant gets herself ready for the next season. Preparation is living, ready for tomorrow's opportunity; it is living in the present with a clear view of the future. This is the reason why someone would attend school in the dead of the winter in spite of a forecasted accumulation of 20 inches of snow; he or she is preparing for the envisaged future.

Why do we need to be prepared?

(1) Success is like a dress rehearsal. The better prepared we are, the better our performance will be on the stage of life. Life is also a school. It does not matter where we are in the university of our lives. God uses the circumstances in our lives to transform and mold us. However, no matter the stage of life in which we find ourselves, there are opportunities to be taken advantage of based on how prepared we are. It is crucial to stress that the worst part of life is to be called unto the stage of life and be found ill-equipped. In order to prosper we must not only focus on the end-results, but we must equally value process and preparation. In essence, God is saying to us through the lesson of the ant – do not be afraid in hard times; they are periods for preparation and fortification for upcoming seasons of our lives.

(2) Preparation also opens doors and windows of opportunities for us. Apostle Paul wrote that everyone who runs in a race runs with the intention of winning. If we are to win, we must be disciplined enough to ready ourselves. Those who will stay on top when the seasons of life change

and those who will win the race of life will be those who are prepared in all seasons. It is therefore worth repeating that we must prepare and plan for our future.

(3) Life comes in stages and we cannot afford to be complacent or resigned to the stage in which we find ourselves. What we do in one stage of our lives prepares us for the next. Also, what we fail to do in one stage will make us unprepared for the next. Opportunities will also arise at that next stage of life but such opportunities will only abound to those who are prepared for it.

(4) Preparation makes us confident when opportunity comes. Opportunities can be intimidating if one is not adequately prepared. However, there is a sense of boldness and confidence that one possesses when you are qualified for a task by reason of preparation.

Joseph is a good example of a man who applied the wisdom of foresight and the virtue of preparation to step into the next stage of his life, as recorded in Genesis 41:29-36. Joseph, through careful planning readied himself and emerged victorious when the winter season of his life was over. In hard times, what guarantees your success and makes you a victor ahead of others is having the right plans.

We must begin to ask ourselves personal questions of this nature; "What plans do I have for my life?" "What plans do I have for my finances and for investments?" "How do I plan my time?" "Do I plan my days, weeks and months or do I allow events to simply highjack my days?" "Do I accomplish my daily goals or do I end up busy doing nothing?" These questions are geared at a subjective and honest analysis of our lives so that our minds can be renewed by the truth we are reading today. This is the only way we can experience changes. Furthermore, the renewal of mind that will bring changes will take deliberate, conscious and prayerful effort. There is no short-cut to prosperity. We must cultivate the right habits because if we leave it to chance, nothing will happen. This mindset albeit usual, must be taught in the Church. Planning and investing is not contrary to the Word of God. Due to Joseph's inspired ideas and wise planning, Pharaoh positioned him to prosper!

There are those who live their lives in a meaningless routine. They wake up, go to work, come back home, and eat. In two weeks they receive their pay check, pay their bills, buy food, clothes, and shoes - and that is it! There is no thought for the future! There are some who place undue value and emphasis on what they wear as assets; yet, what we wear depreciates. We must make good investment plans for our lives like Joseph did. The seven years of plenty cut across the whole land and everyone experienced the surplus but they did not make good plans for their future. Only Joseph did (on behalf of Pharaoh), and as a result he was in control of all things and was master over all in the dry season. We must ask God to open our eyes of understanding at every stage of life, in order to see right, plan right, and live our lives by revelation. That is, we must be able to discern the seasons of our lives. It is not all monies that come our way that should be seen as spending money. Some of it should constitute seed money. Seed money is money meant to be saved because there will be an opportunity for investment in the future. Our goal must not only be to plan right but to seek God-given ideas. Yes, God still gives ideas!

Usually we see that when people ask for a miracle, God gives them directions and instructions, which is what God is doing through this publication. The ability to embrace the miracle is dependent upon our obedience to His instructions. Two examples of this in the Bible are the widow of Zarephath [1 Kings 17:1-16] who with her son was about to die. God sent His prophet Elijah with instructions for her breakthrough, and through her obedience she survived and prospered. There was also another widow, (the wife of the prophet) who was in debt and her sons were to be sold [2 Kings 4:1-4]. Again God sent instructions through His prophet Elisha and through her obedience to God's Word also, she prospered and her sons were delivered from bondage.

Even as we plan, we do not have to pilfer someone else's idea. We must come to the understanding that God will give us our own sanctified spirit-filled ideas for prosperity, if we ask Him. There are still so many Holy Ghost ideas that will lift us. Let us begin to pray in the light of God's Word in Deuteronomy 8:18, that He should open our eyes to opportunities by faith! Faith sees windows where others see walls. Faith sees opportunities and believes that we cannot sink, for it is an undefeatable spirit. Faith does not live by our power but by the power of God; it does not live on our resources but on the resources of Heaven. Faith says if Heaven cannot fail, then we cannot fail. Faith opens our eyes to see the potential, possibilities, and greatness that lie in us.

Faith understands that because the Lord is our Shepherd, we shall not want. God is our divine provider; He is our source and others are merely channels; that is, one source and many channels. When the source is open and flowing like a river, even if one channel is blocked, there is no stopping the deluge of water, which will find outlets at every turn. So, when man closes one door (channel) against you, it should not cause you to panic if you affirm that God, the source, is for you. As long as you are hooked up to the source, it is only a matter of time before another channel bursts open. God is our ready help; wisdom is still flowing from Him; insight and ideas are still coming from Him.

THE LESSON FROM THE CONIES

> *"The conies are but a feeble folk, yet make they their houses in the rocks…* [Proverbs 30:26].

The conies are also known as rock badgers and Arabian or field mice. The conies although tiny and vulnerable have learnt how to prepare for their future by finding security underneath rocks. This means that the conies are skillful at harnessing resources around them. In order to prosper at all times including hard times, like the conies, we must learn to be skillful in harnessing our surrounding resources. A lot of people expend so much time and energy trying to get out of their present condition and environment that they become blinded to the resources around them. They fail to understand that God has positioned resources in that same environment that could form the "launching platform" for their next level.

DIVINE HABITAT

Relocation from one city to another should not always be the initial reaction to any unfavorable condition. Everybody has a spiritual habitat; a place ordained by God for success and breakthrough. We must be content with where we are in order to be properly positioned for where we are going. Being satisfied does not mean that we have resigned to our condition but that we have an inner satisfaction at the current level, not based on things, but on trusting God. Absence of this inner joy at any level can make a person so insecure, ungrateful and bitter. Such a person may fail to appreciate or embrace those that God has positioned around him or her as resources for the next level.

Just like the conies, we must always be skillful at identifying the resources at our disposal - and utilize them. For example, many people would want to have thousands of dollars in-hand before they decide to embark on a project, without regard for their current small-but-steady stream of income. It is time for you to sit down and plan; it is time for husband and wife to plan together and not in opposite directions. The conies are skillful in harnessing resources around them in order to fortify themselves. What are the resources available to you today? God has provided them so you can fortify your destiny with them. We must stop looking at what we do not have and begin to fortify ourselves with what we have.

THE LESSON FROM THE LOCUSTS

> *"The locusts have no king, yet go they forth all of them by bands"* [Proverbs 30:27].

The locusts have no king, no guide, no counselor, no "big brother" and no influential connections, so to speak, to back them up. However, in Joel 2: 25, the Bible refers to the locusts as the armies of God. God also used locusts to punish Pharaoh. Anyone familiar with farming knows that the worst nightmare of a farmer is to have his or her farm invaded by locusts. Where do the locusts derive their strength? It is from the bands that they form in cooperation; it is from the unity they exhibit.

PARTNERSHIP - LEVERAGING RELATIONSHIPS

The lesson to be learnt from the locusts is the power of partnership. It is a known fact that one of the rules of success is building a great team. Success does not require an individual to be an expert in every field; it requires the development of a good network. It is profitable to know your limitations and be able to surround yourself with those who have strengths in your areas of limitation. This is for the purpose of a harmonious coordination of their knowledge and expertise in order to assist one another with achieving individual goals.

We must therefore cultivate the habit of networking with others so as to bring our efforts together to form a unified and effective front. In Ecclesiastes 4:9-12, the Bible states,

> *"Two are better than one; because they have a good reward for their labor. For if they fall, the one will lift up his fellow; but woe to him that is alone when he falleth; for he hath not another to help him up. Again, if two lie together, then they have heat: but how can one be warm alone? And if one prevails against*

> *him, two shall withstand him; and a threefold cord is not easily broken."*

The above scripture is often quoted as justification for marriage but this scripture places more emphasis on the benefits of partnership in any setting. So if you do not want to be stagnant, seek out others with ideas that will take you to the next level.

Speaking mainly to people of color, one of our gravest weaknesses is the inability to work together. We are filled with pride, insecurity, jealousy, envy and a sense of mistrust for one another but, as believers, we must operate differently. We must learn to bond and pull together to achieve greater success. When we bring our resources together, our bargaining and purchasing power increases.

Nehemiah was able to complete the project of rebuilding of the city wall in a record fifty-two days because of the power of networking. Chapter Three of the book of Nehemiah chronicles how the people leveraged the power of networking in completing the wall notwithstanding the opposition from their enemies. God must help us to overcome the crab mentality, which says, "I am not going anywhere and neither will you." God wants us to have the Jesus mentality which says, "Rejoice with them that rejoice." However, it is expedient to mention that we should not simply form partnership(s) on a handshake, based on the fact that we are Brothers-and Sisters-in-the-Lord, or because we have some other form of a comfortable relationship. It is of import that proper legal partnership agreements are drafted by an attorney clearly stating the terms of the agreements for incorporation, daily operations, profit sharing, etc.

Some naysayers might argue that joint ventures are too risky but to that I say, "Life is a risk." That we leave our houses daily, drive cars or ride on the subways are all risks. Many a times, we as believers are willing to believe God for the mundane things of life but when it comes to calculated and profitable risks, we set up a mental road-block that advances negative reasons or opinions on why a beneficial venture will not pan out; that is, be a success. We must be ready and willing to believe God for a risk that could be financially profitable; we must be willing to destroy the grasshopper mentality and be possessed with the spirit of faith and possibility.

THE LESSONS FROM THE SPIDERS

> *"The spider skillfully grasps with its hands, and it is in kings' palaces"* [Proverbs 30:28].

Spiders can be found everywhere - even in a mansion, no matter how clean or immaculate it is. This is because spiders are very ingenious in weaving their webs. One of the lessons to be learnt from the spider is creativity. Prospering at all times requires that we develop a creative mindset. Have we ever pondered on how the Internet came about or how e-mail came into existence? Have we ever paused to consider the invention of airplanes or how simple ideas grow into billion-dollar franchise ventures? It all comes through creativity.

CREATIVITY & DILIGENCE

There are still so many things in the realm of creation that are waiting to be discovered and made manifest for the use of mankind. This will begin to take place as we ask God to sanctify and anoint our minds with creative insight. We cannot afford to waste time by a preoccupation with frivolous things; rather, we must engage our mental power for creative ideas and wisdom. Another lesson to be learnt from the spiders is the lesson of diligence. Not only are the spiders creative, they work with their hands earnestly. Diligence is defined as careful and persistent work or application to an undertaking. It is paying attention to details, refusing to operate with the spirit of mediocrity, and allowing the spirit of excellence to permeate us.

For instance, we are to provide five-star service to our customers in a clean business environment. Gone are the days of engaging in shoddy businesses. We must endeavor to package our business with excellence and be willing to pay the price for the latter. Being the best at what we do requires continuous investment into one's life. Such investment increases our value and worth in the society. The Bible says that a man that is diligent in his business will stand before kings and not mere men. Diligence is a supernatural ladder for promotion and increase.

Not many of us will start our own businesses now but we must be faithful and consistent with whatever we do in our present position. We should persevere and not allow the tide of life to drive us to and fro. We should not become jacks-of-all-trades and master of none; we must master - and become proficient with - our current assignments. Prosperity does not occur in an instant; it takes patience and persistence. Moreover, whatever you are doing right now may later provide the seed for your future endeavors.

Chapter 7

Other Practical Habits of Prosperity

There are other practical habits that should be put into practice in our quest for prosperity so as to prevent any manner of stagnation. A thorough understanding of your proficiencies will enable you to determine habits and actions which you can develop or undertake by yourself and those which will require sound advice from subject matter experts.

Remember that it is God who gives us power to get wealth. So once you are able to access that power, wealth will surely come your way. The Bible warns us that hasty shortcuts lead to poverty. People who are always searching for get-rich-quick schemes often find themselves disappointed. There are also others who though they make a steady income do not know how to increase it, because they do not have an outlook of prosperity. Consequently, we need to cultivate the fundamental habits of working and investing in order to break cycles of failure and mediocrity.

WORKING

This is an aspect of kingdom practices that is sometimes misconstrued and incorrectly represented. Working is erroneously regarded as a consequence of the fall of man, thus giving an impression that it is a curse, which it is absolutely not. God gave Adam the assignment to till the Garden of Eden and also to name all the animals *before* the curse of disobedience was pronounced on mankind. The covenant demands that we work smart, pray, and give tirelessly. Working without giving and praying is working in vain. Similarly, giving and praying without working will prevent the blessings of giving and praying from accruing in your life. Psalms 1:3 states, "…whatsoever he doeth…" So God expects you to be doing something that can provide a platform for which His blessings can accrue in your life. In the covenant, there is no future for the idle man!

Plans are only good intentions unless they are reinforced with hard work. Jesus called most of His disciples while they were at work; for example, fishing or at a tax office. Jesus seemed to like busy, industrious people, commending shrewd stewards that turned a profit. David and Moses were both called when they were out with the sheep; Elisha was called while he was plowing. God's work of redemption and providence continues, so we who are made in His image are likewise created to work. Work is therefore a noble activity and so our work should reflect that of God. God is interested in our work and will supply us with wisdom so we can work effectively and efficiently. His wisdom is practical and craftsmanlike. The person that God gave the greatest power to make wealth was Solomon. However, He did not drop gold bars from heaven for Solomon; rather, He gave him unfathomable wisdom and business acumen. It was this wisdom that enabled Solomon to rule wisely, judge accurately, and make a profit.

> *"So I saw that there is nothing better for a person than to enjoy their work, because that is their lot"* [Ecclesiastes 3:22a, NIV].

Work is a gift from God. Solomon said that we should see our work as a gift from God that gives meaning and purpose to life. For Solomon, doing one's work well and being satisfied with it was central to human satisfaction. This is in contrast to the Greek view of work as a burden for slaves and the masses. Work is to be done diligently and vigorously because it is a major approach through which we can prosper at all times and in all seasons. John Edmonton is accurate in describing work as "the engine of prosperity in a world that will quickly send you broke if you fail to master it, through the concentrated application of applied wisdom in a spirit of excellence."

INVESTING (LET YOUR MONEY WORK FOR YOU)

There are three skill sets necessary for financial prosperity. These are the skill of making money, managing money and also making your money to work for you. Working just to make money is the primary level in financial prosperity; however, it has its limitations. Although it can provide a measure of comfort, it may not necessarily make you prosperous. The art of being overly dependent on just making money especially through salaried employment can be affected by several factors. What happens when you retire? What about the fear of being downsized or terminated from employment? What happens when the person is unable to work for the pay? So instead of depending on just making money, God has graced each and every individual with the wisdom to make your money or trading material work for you. This is known as investing.

In His parable of talents, Jesus advocated investing money rather than just keeping it "under a mattress." He criticized the servant who buried the single talent that was assigned to him, while commending the servants that earned good returns on their investments [Matthew 25]. It seems that learning to make good investment decisions is a key part to creating wealth. Thus, it is imperative you begin to explore the prudent investment of a portion of your accumulated savings. This could be invested in stocks and shares or real estate. Good enough, these avenues of investment can be started with minimal amounts. Investment requires risk taking and my advice is that you start at your own level of comfort. You need to also seek the advice of financial investors in order to maximize your opportunities. In addition to that, it is important to know the biblical principles of investing and equally important, be led by the Spirit as you embark on it.

> *"Cast your bread upon the waters, for you will find it after many days. [2]Give a serving to seven, and also to eight, for you do not know what evil will be on the earth"* [Ecclesiastes 11:1-2].

It is certainly not a good idea to invest your money in a single venture. No investment is guaranteed. Therefore, it is better to diversify your investments so that if one does poorly, the losses you take on that investment will be offset by your gains in other investments. Whether it is choosing a stock to invest in or investing in real estate, choose one where you understand the products and how it makes money. Investing can be a part of your life, but it should not rule your life. If your life revolves around how your investment portfolio is performing, then you need to reassess your priorities. Money can be a defense and should be built up in preparation for the future, but obtaining wealth should never be your only purpose in life.

Many outstanding investment vehicles have been created because of the greediness of man. They offer a pathway to great riches in a short amount of time, but they also offer the chance for great poverty. You should never enter into any type of investment that could cause you to lose more than you originally invest. Due to the fall of man, cycles of economic prosperity do not continue forever. Therefore, you must plan for the inevitable even though as a believer, you hope for the best. This is what made Joseph such a valuable steward to Pharaoh; he was able to create wealth in both the bull and the bear markets of Egypt. Although God wants us to be good stewards of His wealth, the desire for riches should not be the guiding principle of our lives.

> *"But seek first the kingdom of God and His righteousness, and all these things shall be added to you"* [Matthew 6:33].

LEVERAGING DEBT

Leveraging debt is another way to make your money work for you, but the concept of debt has been misunderstood by some. Most people run away from it instead of using it strategically. It is not a sin to borrow money to start a venture especially if you do not have the initial capital. It is a known fact that some rich people rarely use their money, but rather rely on borrowed money to make money!

> *"Now there cried a certain woman of the wives of the sons of the prophets unto Elisha, saying…the **creditor** is come to take unto him my two sons to be bondmen.*
> *2And Elisha said unto her, what shall I do for thee? Tell me, what hast thou in the house? And she said, Thine handmaid hath not anything in the house, save a pot of oil.*
> *3Then he said, Go, **borrow** thee vessels abroad of all thy neighbors, even empty vessels; **borrow** not a few"* [2 Kings 4:1-3, KJV].

Just like the story of the woman in the scripture passage above, it is allowable – and you should be willing – to procure loans for investments in assets that appreciate and not on perishable items or things that depreciate in value. This provides the necessary initial capital which can boost investment opportunities. This is what I call "strategic borrowing;" the strategic usage of debt to build wealth so you can pay off the debt in a given period of time.

I was told the true story of a church "A" in the southern part of U.S.A., in the late 1990s. A church "B" located across the street from church "A" was relocating to their newly constructed building and they offered church "A" the opportunity to assume the mortgage of their current building at a very low interest rate. Church "A's" Board of Trustees quoted Deuteronomy 28:12 and Romans 13:8 as justification for their unwillingness to borrow money. Needless to say, they did not acquire the property despite the fact that they had been praying to God for the provision of such a building for the next phase of their growth and effectiveness. When several attempts to convince them failed, the same offer was made to another church "C." Although God does not rate a church by the size or the beauty of its building, such qualities are sometimes contributing factors to the growth and success of a ministry; and if care is not taken, your building can reduce your vision to its size. The aforementioned church "A" became stagnant and lost membership while church "C" flourished. The latter became the center of attraction within the community for worship, even as the church rendered various services to the community. As God would have it, church "C" grew and paid off the mortgage in a record time, becoming totally debt free.

MULTIPLYING WEALTH (EMBRACING THE OCEANIC DIMENSION OF PROSPERITY)

The ability to become prosperous at all seasons requires having more than one source of income. There is no prosperous or wealthy individual that has only one source of income. Their business may be their only source, but the business itself will generate money from various other sources. So the secret of an ever-increasing, never-running-dry wealth is establishing diverse sources of income.

It is a given fact that irrespective of the season of the year, the ocean never runs dry. While it is possible that small bodies of water such as streams, ponds, and rivers may dry up during the dry seasons in certain parts of the world, seas and oceans never run dry. This is simply because every body of water either from lakes, streams, rivers, ponds, etc., will ultimately find their way and discharge their water into the sea or ocean.

So the secret behind the continuous flow of the ocean is that it receives water from several sources. Therefore, becoming prosperous like an ocean no matter what comes your way, demands that you establish different sources of income. This will ensure that you will never run dry financially, irrespective of the prevailing conditions around you. Just the same way that some streams dry up in the dry season and the ocean remains full, you will remain prosperous even in hard times.

DIMENSIONS OF WEALTH CREATION

There are many different dimensions of wealth creation that are capable of lifting your destiny above any form of recession. These include but are not limited to:

(1) One-time Source. This is the type of wealth flow where you work once and get paid once. In order to get paid again, you have to work again. This includes work such as salaried employment, contracts, sales, etc.

(2) "Once-and-always Source." This is the type of wealth flow that requires you to work hard once, but with continuous payment to you for the initial labor. In this instance, you do not have to work hard again to continue receiving money from this source of wealth. Owning rental properties, writing books and releasing music albums all fall under this category. Jesus paid the price for our salvation once and for all on the cross of Calvary and has since been seated at the right hand of God reaping the eternal harvest of the sacrifice.

> *"For the death that he died, he died to sin once and for all: but the life that he lives, he lives to God"* [Romans 6:10].

(3) Free-flow Source. This is a wealth stream where you make your money work for you. The money does all the work while you enjoy the benefits. Examples of this are stocks, bonds, mutual funds, etc.

WHY MULTIPLE SOURCES OF INCOME?

(1) It Is the Wisest Thing to Do

It is not financial intelligent to have only one source of income, because if anything goes wrong, you will be at a loss. Wisdom demands that you do not focus all your resources on one avenue of success. The sad truth is that there are many people that are one paycheck away from becoming homeless. This is as a result of absolute dependency on one source of income.

(2) It Increases Your Earning Potential

When you have more than one source of income, you earn more money and thus, you increase your revenue. Multiple streams of income undoubtedly have greater earning potential than just one source.

(3) It Reduces and Spreads Your Risks

Having just one stream of income is high risk because if you experience a financial mishap, you might hit rock bottom. However, when you have multiple streams, you spread your risk across your portfolio so that other streams buffer the affected investments, resulting in financial stability.

(4) It Gives You Greater Security

When you have many sources of income, you have greater security because everything simply cannot go wrong in every stream of income at the same time. People with only one stream of income live constantly in fear of losing their job or having dry financial spells, but those with multiple streams are more secure and free from such fears.

(5) It Is the Secret to Unending Wealth and Continuous Prosperity

Just as many rivers flow into the ocean and thus it never runs dry, multiple streams of income represent the source of ocean-like and undiminishing prosperity. There is a continuous in-flow and accumulation of money to great proportions. You make money while you sleep because money now works for you instead of you working for it.

Everybody, from individuals to families, corporations, and even nations, need multiple sources of income. Look within yourself, your family, and nation, and explore the many channels of wealth creation for the activation of multiple streams. Everyone has the potential to have three streams of income as a worst-case scenario, so if you have less than that, you need to make adjustments. Irrespective of the level you are now, you can achieve oceanic dimension of wealth, and no matter how wealthy you already are, you can be wealthier.

Chapter 8

Escaping Poverty Traps

All of the above notwithstanding, we must consistently strive to escape poverty traps which abound every step of the road to prosperity. Irrespective of the times, poverty has no respect for age, race, qualification, location, etc. There are poor people all over the world in different continents. Poverty is not absence of cash, but ignorance of covenant principles for prospering or the discounting of such principles. Every man's poverty is his ignorance. There are several people who are looking for money instead of pursuing covenant principles that will lead to prosperity.

In order to avoid poverty traps and to remain prosperous at all times, it is pertinent to identify the factors responsible for poverty. Several people spend their lives wondering - and searching for - what they can do to be rich and wealthy rather than determining why they are not rich, so as to overcome whatever is preventing them from being prosperous. Regardless of location, poverty exists for many different reasons; we will look at some of them so that we do not fall into such traps.

(1) Stinginess: People tend to develop a culture or lifestyle of hoarding especially during hard times. This may be as a result of fear of insufficiency or to avoid not depleting whatever they have to live on. Although God wants us to be good stewards of the resources He entrusts to our care, covenant practices for prosperity require us to be generous and open to the Holy Spirit for appropriate giving.

> *"There is one who scatters, yet increases more; and there is one who withholds more than is right, But it leads to poverty"* [Proverbs 11:24].

He who gives to advance the cause of the kingdom including caring for the poor will not lack; but he who holds back will not experience the fullness of God's blessing. The attitude of always wanting to receive from others without giving will lead to a closed heaven, and ultimately, poverty. We are not to be reservoirs but channels through which God distributes money and the resources He has entrusted into our hands. We are of course required to withhold a certain portion of our resources such as in savings, but care must be taken to strike a balance between avoiding being stingy and avoiding being a wasteful spender. You must be a kingdom seed sower who knows when to give, where to give and to whom to give. This is usually by the help of the Holy Spirit; however, the Holy Spirit can speak only to those who are open to Him.

(2) Laziness: This is a lifestyle that predisposes you to idleness and procrastination. Some people would rather fold their hands and look unto God's face for instantaneous breakthrough rather praying for ideas or open doors that will constitute a source of income. Anyone who is spiritually or mentally lazy cannot prosper no matter the season.

> *"The lazy man will not plow because of winter; He will beg during harvest and have nothing"* [Proverbs 20:4].

God expects us to develop good work ethics and to work hard so we can break through into a life of plenty. Working hard is not a curse but a commandment from God. If you do not have good work ethics, hard labor will be imposed on you. Laziness is a destroyer of human creativity. There is a dimension of your glory that can only be released when you work creatively. The covenant demands that you work hard, work smart, and work creatively!

(3) Associating with Vain People: When a person is constantly found in the company of people whose value system is contrary to that of the kingdom covenant principles for prosperity, it leads to poverty. Who you follow will determine your destination. Your life is too valuable for you to allow wrong associations to divert your focus.

> *"He that tilleth his land shall have plenty of bread, but he that followeth after vain persons shall have poverty enough"* [Proverbs 28:19, KJV].

We should not be friends with those who waste their resources of time, talent and treasures. God expects you to deliberately and carefully choose those who will have input into your life. Friendship is not by force but by choice. Although we are commanded to love everybody, befriending anyone is a choice. Whoever you associate with, you bear his or her burden. So, it is very important that we select our friends wisely because we eventually become whom we spend time with either to become prosperous or poor. Locate those who can help and guide you into your wealthy place and hook up with them.

(4) Failure to connect with the covenant principles of Tithes & Offerings: Tithing is neither dispensational nor denominational; rather, it is a covenant practice commanded by God. It is also an issue of obedience and every act of obedience commits God's integrity to work on your behalf. Tithing was already in place before the law. God owns a tenth of everything that comes to you. So your tithe is not part of your income, it is God's part of your income!

> *"Will a man rob God? Yet you have robbed Me! But you say, 'In what way have we robbed You?' In tithes and offerings. You are cursed with a curse, for you have robbed Me… Bring all the tithes into the storehouse, That there may be food in My house, and try Me…"* [Malachi 3:8-10].

Many believers are laboring under this curse without conscious knowledge of it. If you are in that category, consider your ways and start tithing today so that you can experience an open heaven. The open heaven is necessary not only for us to have financial increase in our work, but also for us to have ideas that will make money work for us. Working without obedience to covenant principles will always result in laboring in vain. Obedience to covenant principles without working will also not allow any avenue for the blessings of obedience to accrue into your life.

(5) Attitude of Indifference to God's Work: This is the lackadaisical attitude to the work of the kingdom. Prospering at all times requires an attitude that will advance the course of God's kingdom. Many are struggling because they think they can swindle God by not being passionate with His kingdom agenda. One of the primary purposes of salvation is so we can become valuable assets to God's kingdom. Every Christian was delivered from the kingdom of darkness to serve the Living God. When you do otherwise, the toiling continues.

> *"You have sown much, and bring in little; You eat, but do not have enough; You drink, but you are not filled with drink; You clothe yourselves, but no one is warm; And he who earns wages, Earns wages to put into a bag with holes.... Consider your ways! Go up to the mountains and bring wood and build the temple that I may take pleasure in it and be glorified..."* [Haggai 1:6-8].

When you put His kingdom agenda first, God will make you a priority. What really matters is not the amount you give but the heart with which you give. God's favor rests on you when you are a promoter of His cause. For instance, David was a man who was totally committed to the work of God; God responded in kind by preserving David's generation.

(6) Engaging in the Wrong Business: Before Peter met Jesus, he was a professional fisherman all his life. In Luke Chapter Five, whenever he deviated from preaching the gospel, Peter experienced frustration in his fishing business. I am of the opinion that this was because he was in the wrong business that God did not purpose for him. Peter was meant to be in the business of "catching men" rather than in the business of catching fish.

> *"When He had stopped speaking, He said to Simon, 'Launch out into the deep and let down your nets for a catch.' But Simon answered and said to Him, 'Master, we have toiled all night and caught nothing; nevertheless at Your word I will let down the net.' And when they had done this, they caught a great number of fish, and their net was breaking"* [Luke 5:4-6].

After Jesus encountered Simon, He told him that he would no longer catch fish but would catch men - for God. You are not called into every business venture. Locate where you belong because you will only thrive when you do that for which you were wired. If you are not sure, seek direction and good counseling to place you on the right track.

(7) Pride: Some people stay jobless due to pride. They refuse to follow instructions that could deliver them from destruction. Proud people always avoid starting small or starting from where they are, because they have delusions of grandeur. Be very proud of whatever level you are and start at such a level and with whatever resources that you have, no matter how little it is.

> *"Whatever your hand finds to do, do it with your might; for there is no work or device or knowledge or wisdom in the grave where you are going"* [Ecclesiastes 9:10].

We should endeavor to make use of what we have while going after what we want. For instance, when I arrived in the U.S.

in the 1990s, the first job I could get was as a Security Guard out in the bitter cold; but never did I complain. Although I had visions of a brighter and better future, I was willing to proudly start where I was and with what I had. Later on, God promoted me to a position with the State of New York where I rose to management level, and later on to a glorious calling in ministry. Be faithful at the level you find yourself and God will elevate you at the appropriate time.

(8) Living Beyond Your Means: A lifestyle outside of your income will only bring about poverty irrespective of your income level. Several people live to impress others even though it is not convenient for them. They want to look better than everyone, so they keep accumulating unnecessary debt. Prospering at all times including hard times requires an attitude that values the intangibles more than the tangibles. **You must not have a mindset or lifestyle that focuses more on wearing valuables than on becoming more valuable. You are not what you wear!**

> *"He who loves pleasure will be a poor man; He who loves wine and oil will not be rich"* [Proverbs 21:17].

Living life according to the expectations of others is not healthy and will not lead to personal fulfillment. You are not in competition with others; you must align yourself with God's plan for you. Evaluate your life and finances. Have a plan to attain your desired goal(s). Make every effort to carry out your own responsibilities and pray to God always to assist you, because you can do all things through Christ who strengthens you.

(9) Discouragement: Failure in one venture does not make you an outright failure. You may fall several times but you will still rise if you hope in the Lord and are willing to arise by the help of the Holy Spirit. The fact that you are not getting the best in one area of your life now does not mean everything will not fall in place for you. A vision delayed is not a vision denied and a hard time in one season does not mean hard times in all seasons.

> *"Trust in the Lord with all your heart, and lean not on your own understanding; In all your ways acknowledge Him, and He shall direct your paths"* [Proverbs 3:5-6].

Many people have robbed themselves of their destiny because they have allowed discouragement to rob them of their dreams. Discouragement is a thief and a robber of destiny. It is beneficial to live a life of joy and always encourage yourself in the Lord no matter what. Surround yourself with worship songs and anointed sermons. Develop an attitude of gratitude such that when life seems not to be going your way, you do not shut down, but rather, you continually praise God. Such covenant practices grant you access to God's presence where the light of direction will come to guide you.

(10) Not Honoring and Caring for Ministers of God: God's ministers are to be well taken care of because they are His representatives on earth. They are not meant to solicit for money or other resources, but are to be honored. We are not only to honor them with our substance but also to speak well of - and also pray for - them.

> *"He who receives a prophet in the name of a prophet shall receive a prophet's reward. And he who receives a righteous man in the name of a righteous man shall receive a righteous man's reward"* [Matthew 10:41].

Most times, our blessing depends on our willingness to sacrificially care for Ministers of God. For example, there was a time when the Holy Spirit prompted me to sow a seed of $10,000 on behalf of our ministry into the ministry of a man of God who has been a great blessing to us personally and also to our ministry. Then, the heavens opened upon us in a higher dimension because subsequently, a multiple of $10,000 was sown into our ministry. The principle works! It is the anointing that you respect that you can receive from. Do not buy into the philosophy that does not want the ministers of God to be blessed. It is a demonic philosophy.

> *"Soon afterward Jesus began a tour of the nearby towns and villages, preaching and announcing the Good News about the Kingdom of God. He took his twelve disciples with him, along with some women who had been cured of evil spirits and diseases. Among them were Mary Magdalene, from whom he had cast out seven demons; Joanna, the wife of Chuza, Herod's business manager; Susanna; and many others who were contributing from their own resources to support Jesus and his disciples"* [Luke 8:1-3, NLT].

The Bible states clearly here that many devoted their resources in support of Jesus' ministry to reciprocate the blessings they received. If Jesus needed to be supported, so should every Minister of God.

(11) Demonic Activities: Most of the happenings in the physical sometimes have their roots in the spirit realm and poverty in the lives of many is not an exception. There are territorial forces responsible for failure in life, ministry and business. Mammon, the demonic power that controls money causes the spirit of poverty to attack the human race, particularly Christians, with the intent to render them stagnant in all of their endeavors.

> *"And they overcame him by the blood of the Lamb and by the word of their testimony, and they did not love their lives to the death"* [Revelation 12:11].

However, you can overcome these forces through the power in the blood of Jesus and the blessings that flows from an obedient life. Whenever you move to a new place for business or ministry, it is imperative that you gain control over the forces in charge of the terrain, so that you are not limited. Daniel was unable to succeed in Babylon until he broke the power of the prince of Persia. You and I are better equipped than Daniel because the power of resurrection is at work in us. Take up your authority in Christ so you can prevail over forces that may want to oppress your life.

(12) Engaging in Secret Sins: Sin hinders blessings and diminishes one's glory. Sin stops God from working in your life. Perpetuating a sin in secret without confessing and forsaking such a sin will only lead to an impoverished life.

"Behold, the Lord's hand is not shortened, that it cannot save; nor His ear heavy, that it cannot hear. But your iniquities have separated you from your God; and your sins have hidden His face from you, So that He will not hear" [Isaiah 59:1-2].

No sin is too small; sin is sin. God is a good Father who cares for His children and listens to them. Renounce your sins and begin to live according to the covenant. He is not against you having money but He does not want money to control you. Having money is just a part of God's blessing. It is important that you align with the covenant so that you can experience the totality of the blessing. How? Through meditation on His Word, we are enabled to live a lifestyle of the blessing without exerting too much effort.

"Blessed is the man who walks not in the counsel of the ungodly, nor stands in the path of sinners, nor sits in the seat of the scornful; But his delight is in the law of the Lord, and in His law he meditates day and night. He shall be like a tree Planted by the rivers of water, That brings forth its fruit in its season, Whose leaf also shall not wither; and whatever he does shall prosper" [Psalm 1:1-3].

Finally, in order to become truly wealthy and prosperous in all seasons, you need to open your mind to new ideas and develop the skills to take on possibilities greater than your current abilities. It is almost impossible to become wealthy from a perception of lack and limitation because your thoughts become your reality. Successful and prosperous people have the habit of thinking differently from the average person. What stops many people from becoming successful and prosperous is not what they know or do not know. It is their wrong thought pattern that prevents them from moving forward. They speak the language of doubt and unbelief such as, "That is beyond my means," "I can't do that," "I tried it once and it didn't work," "That is impossible," etc. Success demands that whatever season you are in, you must engage in the following: Think prosperously! Work hard! Work smart! Sow prosperously!

It is my hope that this book will serve as a wake-up call and help people in making the decision not to remain sleeping giants. Stop making excuses and set yourself in agreement with God in accomplishing His purpose for you. Ask yourself the following questions. "Am I underutilizing my potential?" "Am I making excuses for failures?" "Am I ready to rise above mediocrity and attain a greater level of excellence and effectiveness?"

A change of mind will ultimately result in a change in situation, in all seasons. It is my entreaty that God through the help of the Holy Ghost will begin to renew our minds in the area of prosperity, for if our minds are renewed, no one will be able to stop us from prospering! Arise today and shine, for your light has come! Activate and put to work the creative grace and the deposit of wisdom presently dormant inside of you. Rise above the tide of lack and want around you so you can begin to flourish and enjoy the best of the land. Change your mindset and language from that of lack and want to that of abundance, possibilities and overflow!

Shalom!

Notes & Reflections

The Greatest Prayer of a Lifetime

The greatest prayer of a lifetime is to be reconnected back to God in a living relationship. Relationship is the basis for asking. You cannot pray to a God who you do not know and who does not know you. God wants to be intimate with you. This type of relationship is available to each one of us when we sincerely repent of our sins, and ask God's forgiveness, and receive His Son, Jesus, as our personal Lord and Savior. If you have never surrendered your life to God, or if you have turned away from God and you want to return to Him, now is the time. God is waiting for you. His arms are open wide to receive you. Just pray this simple prayer right now:

O Lord, be merciful to me, a sinner. I realize that I am a sinner. I need a savior and you are my savior. I repent of every sin, every wrongdoing, and I ask for your forgiveness. I receive Jesus Christ, Your only begotten Son, as my Lord and my Savior. I believe that Jesus went to the cross for me and paid the price for my salvation, and now I receive Him into my heart. I declare that I am born again. I am a child of God. Old sins are gone, and I have a brand-new life in Christ in Jesus' name. Amen.

Contact Information

For more information, feel free to contact Dr. Festus Adeyeye. Although he cannot respond personally to all correspondence, he would love to receive your feedback.

Dr. Festus Adeyeye
Abundant Life Christian Center
Winners' House
32 East 98th Street
Brooklyn
New York 11212
USA

Website: www.alccwinnershouse.org
Phone: 718-566-2601
E-mail: DrFestus@alcministries.com

Twitter: twitter.com/pastor_festus
Facebook: facebook.com/festus.adeyeye

You can order additional copies of this book @

www.alccwinnershouse.org
www.amazon.com
www.barnesandnoble.com

Also By Dr. Festus Adeyeye

Pathways to Breakthrough

Everybody needs to breakthrough in life; from a homeless person on the street who needs a befitting shelter and a change of destiny, to a rich and successful man who may be vying for the presidency of his nation, to a corporate executive who desires elevation on the corporate ladder. In all of these cases breakthrough is needed. Genuine and lasting breakthrough is not what you hop around looking for.

It lies in having a proper understanding of the worth of redemption and laying hold on God's ways of doing things. In this book, you will discover timely truths that will transform your life and cause you to enjoy ever-increasing life in Christ. You will discover that redemption has repositioned you into a new life of power and influence beyond any earthly limitation.

21 Days Prayer Devotional

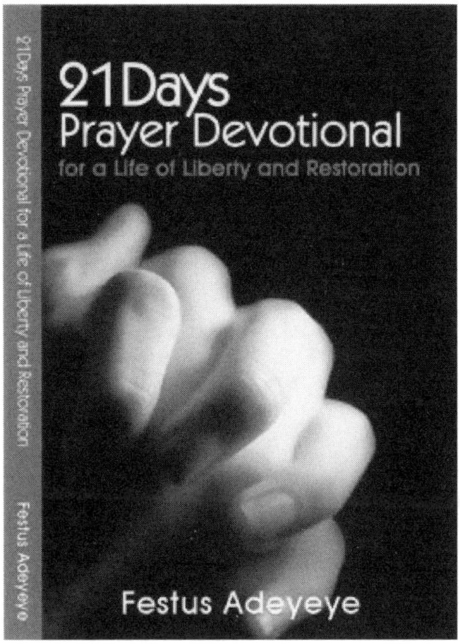

Your perception of each day of your life begins with whom you reflect on daily. No man will be able to despise your face if you see God's face before that of man. Prayer is not a ecclesiastical privilege of some selected people, but a forceful and fervent act for all, in the face of impossibility.

It is an act that is possible for whosoever will accept the challenge of learning how to pray. Human suffering only receives heaven's attention, when a man can initiate prayer here on earth. This *21 Days Prayer Devotional* for a Life of Liberty and Restoration is guaranteed to secure heaven's attention for a radical change in your life!

The Power of Vision

The Power Of Vision is a thought-provoking book that explores the importance of seeing with the eyes of your spirit. Real life begins with vision. In absence of vision, living is reduced to mere existence. Vision will turn a dwarf into a giant; vision will turn the fearful into the bold-hearted.

With vision in his hands, Moses turned from a fugitive into a man with audacity; a run-away became a threat to the powerful king Pharaoh. One man with vision is stronger than a nation, especially when the vision is God-given. How you see and what you see determines your future, and as you read this book, your eyes will be opened to behold wondrous things!

The Prevailing Power of Fasting

The secret to being powerful in the public is to be powerful in your secret. Many are weak in their secret and want to be powerful in the public. This has led to the demise of great potential and great minds. It has led to the demise of great leaders and great dynasties and empires. In order to command power in the public, you must be willing to be strong in your secret.

Jesus performed several miracles daily in the open; however, He spent most of his private life in the presence of God on the mountain. His public ministry was an outflow of the abundance of his discipline and fellowship with his Father in the secret. There is nothing that empowers a man for public command of power and influence like a gaining mastery over himself in the secret. Fasting is that personal spiritual discipline engaged upon in the secret that confers public authority. This is your hour to engage in this glorious adventure that will launch your destiny to a new dimension of power, greatness and honor.